The Story of
Easter
for Children

Book Design
and Illustration:
Erv Gnat

Ideals Publishing Corporation
Milwaukee, Wisconsin

ISBN 0-8249-8076-X

Do you know why we celebrate Easter?

We celebrate this special day
Because the spring has come,
And all the plants come back to life
When wintertime is done.

The rains of spring melt winter snow
And help leaves sprout on trees.

The warm sun helps the grass to grow
And flowers bloom for bees.

A fuzzy caterpillar turns
Into a butterfly.

From eggs hatch tiny baby birds
That chirp up at the sky.

A cute and cuddly kitten's born
That soon begins to purr
Whenever mother gives a bath
And gently licks its fur.

Springtime and Easter bring us joy;
We're joyful for two reasons;
We're thankful Christ rose from the dead
And for the change of seasons.

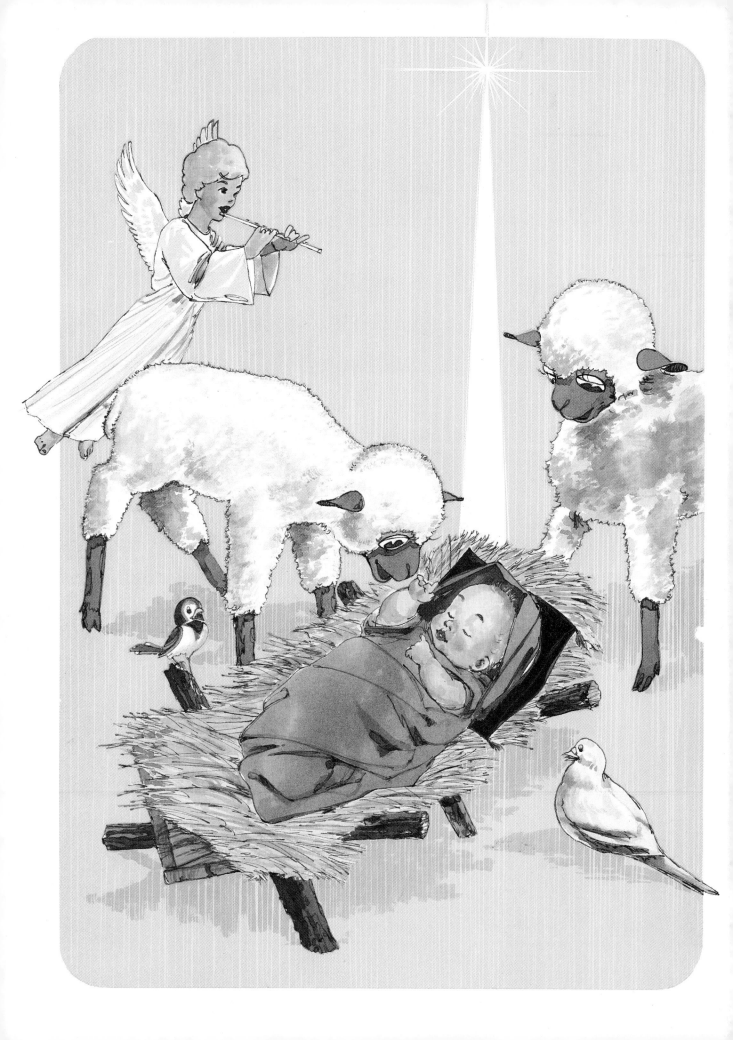

On Christmas Day we celebrate
The day God's Son was born.
He brought us everlasting life
On that first Easter morn.

When he was older, Jesus healed
The sick, the blind, the lame.
His followers were many,
And they proudly spoke his name.

Palm Sunday he rode into town
Upon a donkey's back.
The people sang, "Hosanna, Lord!
You are the king we lack."

Then people laid their clothes and palms
Upon the dusty ground.
To honor Jesus Christ, the Lord,
They gathered all around.

But some men did not like the Lord.
They thought they had the power
To capture him and cause his death,
To bring his final hour.

They put him on a wooden cross
And left him there to die.
His friends were not allowed to help.
They silently stood by.

At dawn on that first Easter Day
His friends went to his tomb,
And by the light of golden day,
They found an empty room.

An angel stood beside the door.
The stone was rolled away.
"The Lord is risen," the angel said,
"He is alive today!"

Christ Jesus rose up from the dead,
A blessing God has given.
We, too, will have life after death
Because his Son has risen.

All Christians go to church today
To celebrate and sing.
They praise the Son of God and say,
"He is our Lord and King!"

The new life given beasts and plants,
Or our lives through God's Son:
The Easter symbols that we see
Can stand for either one.

We see the cross on churches
And their steeples high above.
Since Christ died on a cross for us,
They stand for Jesus's love.

The Easter lily blooms in spring
And stands for Christ's rebirth.
As Jesus rose up from his tomb,
It rises from the earth.

Our Jesus is the Lamb of God.
He's peaceful, pure, and mild.
He is our own Good Shepherd who
Keeps watch on every child.

The Easter eggs you decorate
Mean new life. And in spring
New life appears: chicks hatch from eggs,
New birds arrive and sing.

New bunnies in their burrows
Show new life springs all around.
Some say a rabbit hides the eggs;
We search until they're found.

On Easter Sunday everyone
Wears pretty, lighter clothes.
The earth is clothed with new green grass
Instead of winter snows.

So now on Easter morning when
The birds begin to sing,
You'll sing along in happiness
To warmly welcome spring.

You'll know that Jesus gave to us
The best thing he could give.
He gave us life and rose from death
So that we, too, can live.